771 Wr
WRI Al
c.1 a
a

All You Need To Know About

Making Memory Albums

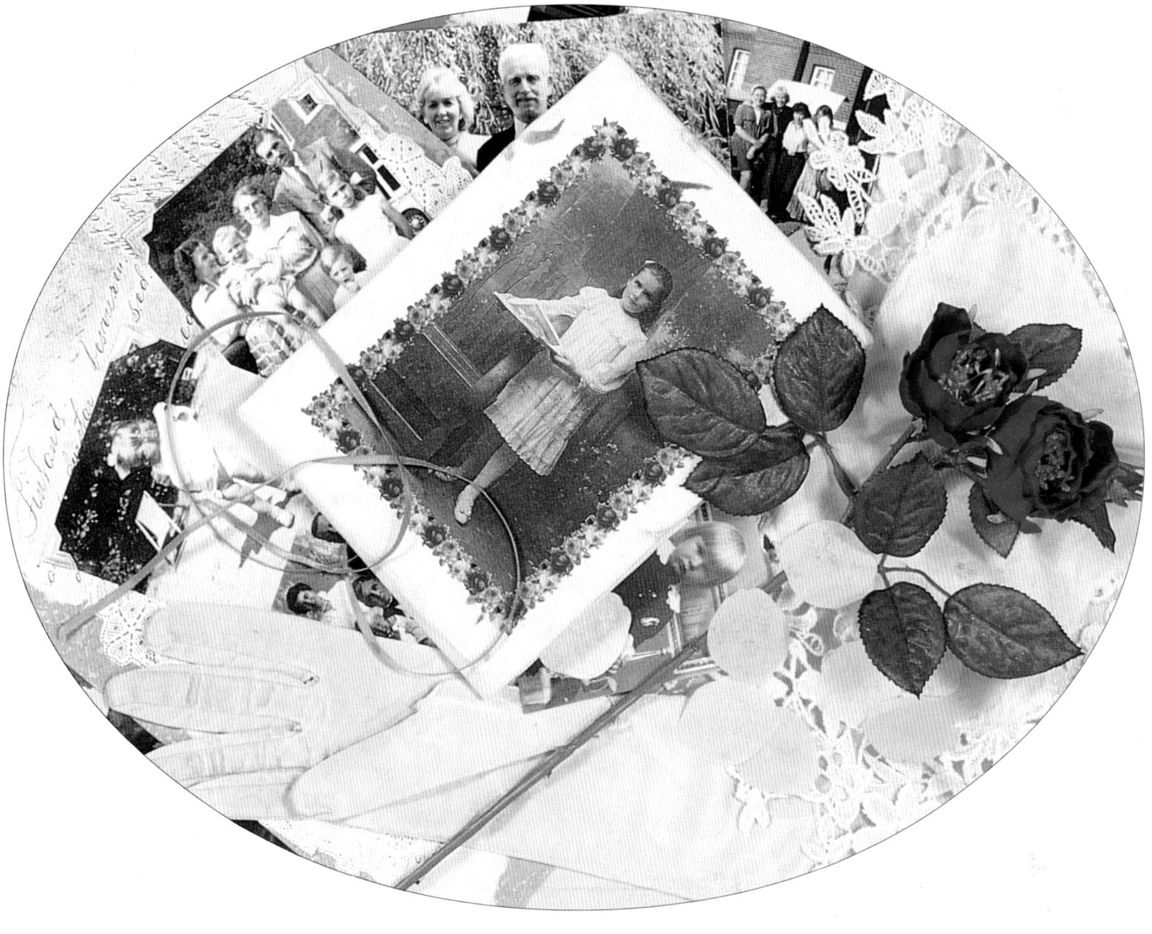

DRIFTWOOD LIBRARY
OF LINCOLN CITY
801 S.W. Highway 101
Lincoln City, Oregon 97367

In memory of my father whom I loved dearly . . .

. . . and to my mother who is always there for me.

ALL YOU NEED TO KNOW ABOUT

MAKING MEMORY ALBUMS

MAGGIE WRIGHT

SEARCH PRESS

First published in Great Britain 1998

Search Press Limited
Wellwood, North Farm Road,
Tunbridge Wells, Kent TN2 3DR

Text copyright © Maggie Wright 1998

Photographs by Search Press Studios
Photographs and design copyright © Search Press Ltd. 1998

All rights reserved. No part of this book, text, photographs or illustrations may be reproduced or transmitted in any form or by any means by print, photoprint, microfilm, microfiche, photocopier or in any way known or as yet unknown, or stored in a retrieval system, without written permission obtained beforehand from Search Press.

ISBN 0 85532 872 X

Readers are permitted to reproduce any of the items/patterns in this book for their personal use, or for purposes of selling for charity, free of charge and without the prior permission of the Publishers. Any use of the items/patterns for commercial purposes is not permitted without the prior permission of the Publishers.

The publishers and author can accept no legal responsibility for any consequences arising from the information, advice or instructions given in this publication.

Suppliers

If you have any difficulty in obtaining any of the materials and equipment mentioned in this book, then please write to the Publishers, at the address above, for a current list of stockists, which includes firms who operate a mail-order service.

Publisher's note

All the step-by-step photographs in this book feature the author, Maggie Wright, demonstrating how to make and decorate a memory album. No models have been used.

DRIFTWOOD LIBRARY
OF LINCOLN CITY
801 S.W. Highway 101
Lincoln City, Oregon 97367

771
WRI
c1

Colour separation by P&W Graphics, Singapore
Printed in Spain by Elkar S. Coop. Bilbao 48012

ING 10^65 12-15-98

The author would like to thank Julie Hickey for her endless enthusiasm and help with the projects and journaling in this book. She would also like to thank Sandy Turner for her help with the decorative finishes on the albums; Judy Balchin for her lettering and for designing the 'Memories' stamps; Ghislaine Frith for designing the parchment craft project; Caroline Childs for being such a wonderful dogsbody; and to a great team of friends who have supplied their treasured photographs and ideas.

Special thanks also go to:

Applicraft, Hillcrest, Guildford Road, Ottershaw, Surrey, KT16 0QL, UK

Blankers, 4 Durham Way, Heath Park, Honiton, Devon, EX14 8SQ, UK

Co-motion Rubber Stamps Inc., 2711 East Elvira Road, Tucson, Arizona, 85707, USA

Deja Views TM, 6 Britton Drive, Box 356, Bloomfield, Connecticut, 06002, USA

Fiskars UK, Bridgend Business Centre, Bridgend, Mid Glamorgan, CF31 3XJ, UK

The Gifted Line, Point Richmond, California, 94804, USA

Hot off the Press Inc., 1250 N.W. Third, Dept. B, Canby, Oregon, 97013, USA

Kuretake Zig Pens, Kuretake UK Limited, 10 Moons Park, Burnt Meadow Road, Redditch, Worcestershire, B98 9PA, UK

Lasting Impressions, 585 West 2600 South, Suite A, Bountiful, Utah, 84010, USA

Making Memories, PO Box 1188, Centerville, Utah, 84014, USA

Penny Black, PO Box 11496, Berkeley, California, 94712, USA

Pentel (Stationery) Limited, Hunts Rise, South Marston Park, Swindon, Wiltshire, SN3 4TW, UK

Pergamano™ UK, Curzon Road, Chilton Industrial Estate, Sudbury, Suffolk, CO10 6XW, UK

Personal Stamp Exchange, 360 Sutton Place, Santa Rosa, California, 95607, USA

Plaid, Box 7600, Norcross, Georgia, 30091, USA

Ranger Industries, 15 Park Road, Tinton Falls, New Jersey, 07724, USA

Rubber Stampede, Ashburton Industrial Estate, Ross-on-Wye, Herefordshire, HR9 7BW, UK

Sakura, Unit 5, The Griffon Centre, Vale of Leven Industrial Estate, Dumbarton, G82 3PD, UK

Stampendous, 1357 South Lewis Street, Anaheim, California, 92805, USA

Stone Marketing Limited, 4 Ashby's Yard, Medway Wharf Road, Tonbridge, Kent, TN9 1RE, UK

Tsukineko Inc., 15411 NE 95th Street, Redmond, Washington, 98052, USA

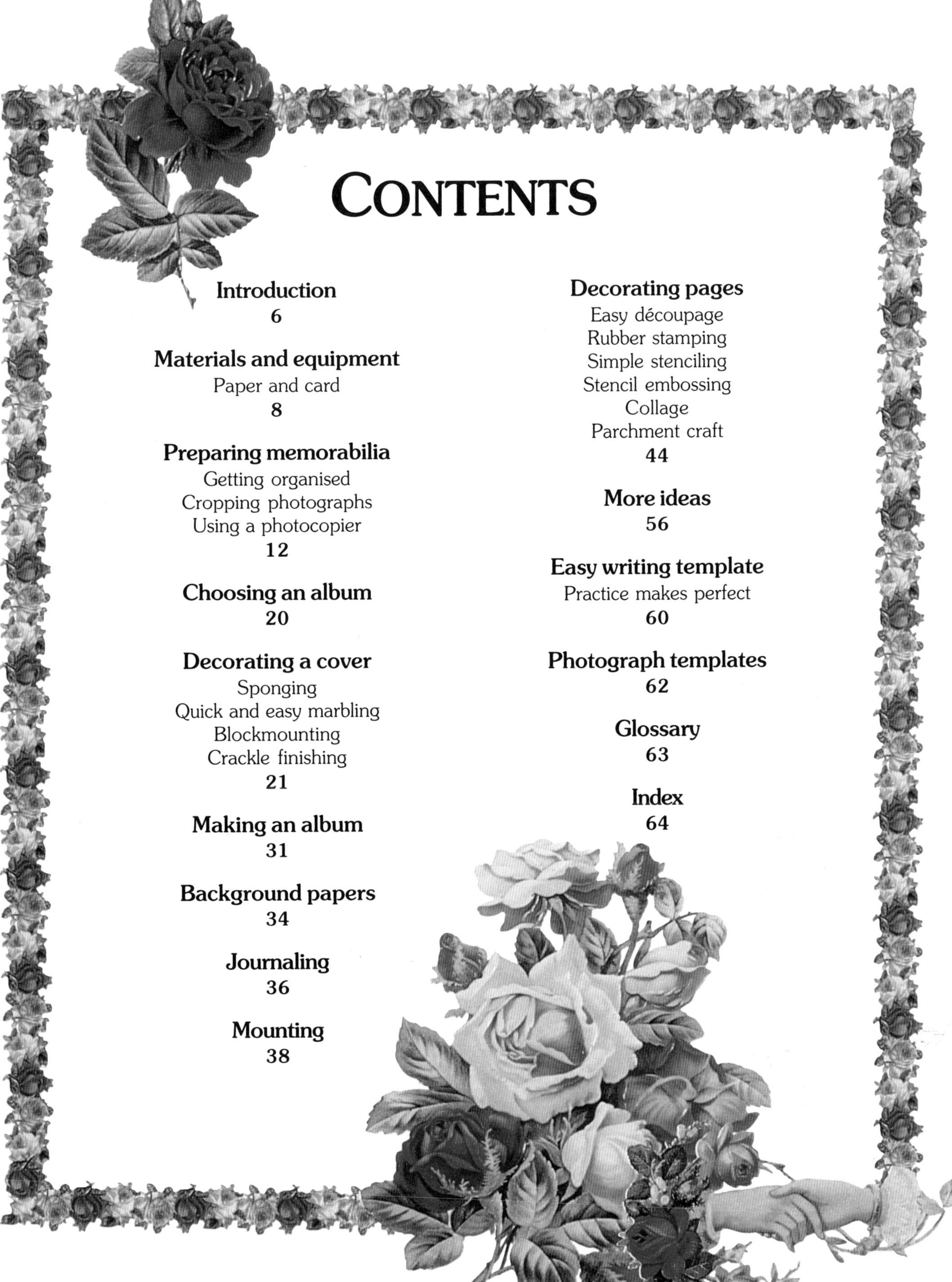

Contents

Introduction
6

Materials and equipment
Paper and card
8

Preparing memorabilia
Getting organised
Cropping photographs
Using a photocopier
12

Choosing an album
20

Decorating a cover
Sponging
Quick and easy marbling
Blockmounting
Crackle finishing
21

Making an album
31

Background papers
34

Journaling
36

Mounting
38

Decorating pages
Easy découpage
Rubber stamping
Simple stenciling
Stencil embossing
Collage
Parchment craft
44

More ideas
56

Easy writing template
Practice makes perfect
60

Photograph templates
62

Glossary
63

Index
64

INTRODUCTION

I often think it would be wonderful to be able to turn back the clock and have a conversation with our ancestors. Although this is not possible, we can communicate with future generations by leaving photographs, mementoes and handwriting to tell a story.

There are few things as beautiful and pleasurable as our treasured memories, but so many of us hide our old photographs and memorabilia away in cardboard boxes once we have looked at them. What could be better than a memory album, where all this can be displayed along with our personal thoughts and feelings.

'But where do I start?' you cry!

This book aims to provide all the information you need to produce a fabulous album. It takes you through all the stages, from theming, cropping and mounting your photographs to choosing your album. It even shows you how to make your own album from card, and how to decorate the cover using a variety of techniques, such as sponging, marbling, crackle finishing and blockmounting.

Background papers can really help to complement your memorabilia, and I give suggestions on how to create your own papers using simple techniques such as rubber stamping and stenciling. I have also included many ideas for decorating your themed pages using, for instance, easy découpage, stencil embossing, collage and parchment craft.

Journaling can provide the finishing touch to an album page, and I give examples of exciting ways to do this. I have even included an alphabet at the back of the book which you can work from, or you can experiment to create your own unique lettering.

A memory album is a wonderful way of preserving your memories, but it is also the perfect gift. So, the next time you are at a family get-together, a special birthday party, a christening or wedding, you can collect memorabilia and take photographs that can then be transformed into a stunning album that will recapture the event forever.

So, now the fun begins – start sorting through those cardboard boxes and go for it!

Maggie Wright

Reached My Heart.
singer fair,
at her feet,
love, the old, old theme,
low and

MATERIALS AND EQUIPMENT

You do not need all the materials and equipment shown here to create your own memory album. However, this photograph shows all the items featured in the book, with the exception of the papers. Many of the materials are acid- and lignin-free – this is to prevent damage to photographs. Materials used for album front covers do not necessarily have to be acid-free (see page 31).

1. **Crackle glaze**: a two-part medium used for crackle finishing.

2. **PVA glue:** can be used as an alternative to glaze medium, for sealing, varnishing and gluing.

3. **White and gold waterproof ink**: used with a mapping pen for parchment craft.

4. **Oil-based varnish**: for sealing non-water-based finishes.

5. **White spirit**: for cleaning brushes used with oil-based products.

6. **Glaze medium**: for sealing, varnishing and gluing.

7. **Metallic spray paints**: for marbling.

8. **Adhesive stick**: for sticking down paper.

9. **Thin acid-free double-sided tape**: for sticking down photographs.

10. **Metallic felt-tip pens**: for detailing, journaling and decorating borders.

11. **Mapping pen**: for tracing patterns on to parchment craft paper.

12. **Single needle tool**: for perforating the edge of parchment craft paper.

13. **Embossing tool**: for use with brass or plastic stencils when embossing.

14. **Embossing mat**: for working on when embossing for parchment craft.

Keep materials and equipment away from photographs while working, to prevent them from getting damaged.

15. **Parchment craft scissor**: for snipping through parchment paper after using a single needle tool.

16. **Decorative scissors**: for creating decorative edges around photographs and mounts.

17. **Decorative punches**: for punching out images such as hearts and stars.

18. **Masking tape**: for holding paper in place (especially useful when stenciling).

19. **Strong double-sided tape**: for use when covering an album.

20. **Single hole punch**: for punching holes when making an album.

21. **Photograph corners**: for mounting photographs on to album pages.

22. **Cutting mat**: for working on when cutting with a craft knife or scalpel.

23. **Craft knife or scalpel**: for cutting out, especially difficult shapes.

24. **General purpose scissors**: for cutting paper.

25. **Foam brush**: for applying paint, varnish etc. These should be kept in a plastic bag to avoid drying out while you work, and should be washed thoroughly after use.

26. **No. 4 round paintbrush**: for painting fine decoration.

27. **Acid-free coloured pens**: for highlighting and journaling.

28. **Ruler**: for measuring and for painting straight edges.

29. **Plastic eraser**: for erasing pencil and chinagraph lines.

30. **Pencil**: for drawing.

31. **Coloured pencils**: for general decoration. These can be used over rubber stamped images.

32. **Chinagraph pencil**: for marking photographs before cropping. The line will rub off.

33. **Sandpaper**: for sanding gift wrap in the blockmounting technique.

34. **Paper towel**: for mopping up and pressing out air bubbles from glued images.

35. **Surgical gloves**: for protecting hands when sponging and marbling. These allow you more dexterity than conventional rubber gloves. They are available from chemists.

36. **Plastic stencils**: for stenciling.

37. **Templates**: for cropping photographs.

38. **Dried flowers, tassels, metallic thread, buttons**: for adding decoration.

39. **Acid-free stickers**: for adding decoration in the easy découpage technique.

40. **Ribbon**: for attaching an album spine and for adding decoration.

41. **Needles**: for threading ribbon through an album spine.

42. **Ink pad**: for use with rubber stamps.

43. **Rubber stamps**: for stamping.

44. **Lightbox**: for stencil embossing.

45. **Brass stencils**: for stenciling and stencil embossing.

46. **Sponge dauber**: for use with an ink cube when stenciling.

47. **Ink cubes**: for stenciling and stencil embossing.

48. **Glitter glue**: for adding sparkle to your work.

49. **Paint**: acrylic paint is used for decorating album covers. Oil-based paint is used for bringing up the cracks in the crackle finishing technique.

50. **Natural or synthetic sponge**: for sponging an album cover.

51. **Paper plate**: for use as a paint palette.

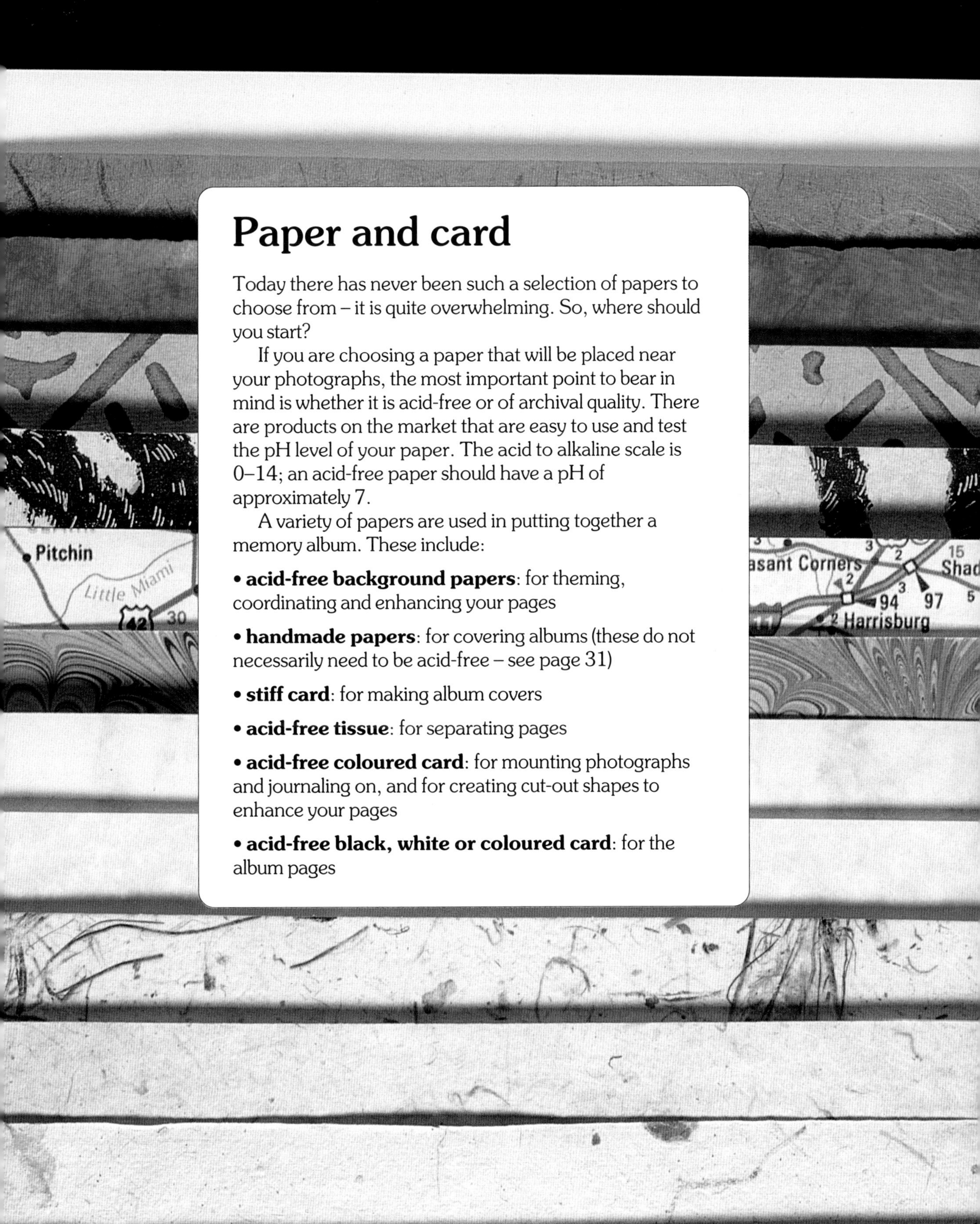

Paper and card

Today there has never been such a selection of papers to choose from – it is quite overwhelming. So, where should you start?

If you are choosing a paper that will be placed near your photographs, the most important point to bear in mind is whether it is acid-free or of archival quality. There are products on the market that are easy to use and test the pH level of your paper. The acid to alkaline scale is 0–14; an acid-free paper should have a pH of approximately 7.

A variety of papers are used in putting together a memory album. These include:

- **acid-free background papers**: for theming, coordinating and enhancing your pages
- **handmade papers**: for covering albums (these do not necessarily need to be acid-free – see page 31)
- **stiff card**: for making album covers
- **acid-free tissue**: for separating pages
- **acid-free coloured card**: for mounting photographs and journaling on, and for creating cut-out shapes to enhance your pages
- **acid-free black, white or coloured card**: for the album pages

PREPARING MEMORABILIA

First of all, gather together all the photographs, cuttings and postcards you have hidden away in that old box or drawer. Start by sorting everything into themes, i.e., a memorable family get-together, a special birthday party, the holiday of a lifetime, a baby's christening or an unforgettable wedding. If you have any special mementos from the events, you should include these as well. For example, tickets from the theatre, wine bottle labels from that special occasion, airline tickets or even the first lock of hair from your baby all make excellent additions to the pages, depending on the theme.

ASTORIA CAPSIS HOTEL – IRAKLION – GR
ATHENS
OMONIAS
PLATEIA
PATISSION
ΑΡΧΑΙΟΤΗΤΕΣ
ΤΗΣ ΕΛΛΑΔΟΣ
ΙΕΡΟΝ
ΔΕΛΦΩΝ
ΜΔ
451870
ΔΡΧ 30
Α. Π.
ΕΙΣΟΔΟΝ
ΜΔ 451870
ΔΕΛΦΟΙ: ΜΟΥΣΕΙΟΝ–ΙΕΡΟΝ
ΕΙΣΙΤΗΡΙΟΝ

Getting organised

Now your photographs and memorabilia are sorted into themes, you should file each theme into an acid-free plastic protector, then store in a ring binder. Alternatively, you could place each themed selection into an acid-free envelope and then store in a storage box. Always try to store photographs in a room you use on a day-to-day basis – attics and basements are often too damp and cold.

Select all the photographs and mementoes you want to use in your album, then decide what you want to go on each page. Place each page into an envelope or transparent file, and reference it clearly. It is a good idea to keep simple notes to help you remember details. For each photograph, it is worth recording the date it was taken, where it was taken, the names of the people in it and the reason for taking the photograph.

Always wash your hands thoroughly before handling photographs, to remove any trace of handcreams or oils.

Any mementoes that are not acid-free can be colour photocopied, encased in clear acid-free envelopes, or even laminated.

Do not discard photographs that have 'red eyes' in them. There are special pens that can be purchased to remove the unwanted colour.

Photographs should be organised into themed groups.

Cropping photographs

Photographs often contain too much unwanted background, which detracts from the main subject . . . but we are all terrified to cut into our treasured photographs! However, nowadays you can have your photographs colour photocopied (see page 18) and you can then crop these reproductions. Alternatively, for only a little extra cost you could request a duplicate set of prints, and you can crop those. In this way, your original stays intact.

You should never crop a polaroid photograph, as acid can seep out when it is cut.

When cropping, you may find it easier to move the photograph and not the scissors.

The photograph on the left is cropped, leaving the house and car to show the scale and height of the wave. If the house and the car are left out of the photograph, you lose a sense of scale and the waves do not look as dramatic (see right).

Plastic templates can be used to help you crop photographs. They are readily available and come in a selection of different shapes and sizes, including ovals, circles, squares and rectangles as well as more elaborate shapes such as hearts, stars and bells.

Use a chinagraph pencil to draw around the template, as this can be rubbed off with a plastic eraser and will not damage the photograph. The photograph can then be cut out carefully with a sharp pair of scissors or a craft knife.

The original photograph

The wrong way to crop
Notice how much sand is left in the picture, which detracts from the central image of the parachute and the figures.

The right way to crop *The extraneous background and foreground has been cropped out, placing the focus very clearly on the parachute and the figures.*

The original photograph

The wrong way to crop
Notice how, by cropping out the parachute, the photograph loses meaning and colour.

The right way to crop
The parachute has been included, adding colour and making the picture more understandable. The portrait oval shape complements the elements in the photograph.

Opposite
Fun in the sun
This album page shows cropped photographs mounted on a themed background paper of sand dunes. The parachute is made out of coloured card and strings have been drawn in so that they link up with the strings in the central photograph.

Tunisia
HELP!
You call this a vacation?
Derek and Vicky on the brave side paraglidin from the beach in Tunisia
Summer 1992

Using a photocopier

Photographs can get damaged over time, and colour photographs, no matter how carefully you look after them, will fade eventually. If you are unhappy about using original photographs, have them photocopied – in either black and white or in colour.

You can also photocopy a photograph if you are nervous about cropping (see page 15) – you can then crop that image rather than the original.

You can use a photocopier to enlarge or reduce the size of a photograph, and you can use duplicates of different sizes to decorate a page. Alternatively, if you still possess your negatives, you can order new prints in various sizes.

Precious photographs that are slightly torn or have been damaged by silver fish, for example, can be taken to a professional photographic shop to be restored.

An image in a magazine will not usually be acid-free. If you want to use it in your album, you should use a colour photocopy of the image.

Original black and white photograph
Try to take at least one roll of black and white film a year of the family. Black and white photographs outlast colour ones, and will allow you to have photographs to hand down to future generations.

Black and white photocopy
You can preserve a black and white photograph by having it photocopied. You can also photocopy a colour photograph in black and white.

Sepia photocopy
Some photocopiers have a function which enables you to change the colour of the ink to produce a sepia photocopy of a black and white photograph.

Original sepia photographs are enhanced by colour photocopying, and in some cases they are even better than the originals!

A sepia photocopy of a black and white photograph is here mounted on card and edged with paperlace. The mount is then built up using layers of coordinating background card and papers.

Choosing an Album

You can buy a photograph album or journal from craft suppliers and personalise it; or create your own from card, paper and ribbon; or make one using a kit of specially designed materials that are readily available from art and craft shops. The latter need to be assembled following the manufacturers' instructions. Whichever you choose, the album cover can be easily decorated to give a stunning look.

If you are buying an album, you should first decide what shape and size you want it to be. It is possible to buy both landscape and portrait shapes in a wide variety of sizes – you can even purchase miniature ones. Expandable albums and ringbinders are also available and these are extremely popular because pages can be added easily at a future date. However, it is important to check that extra pages are easily available when buying these types of album.

Prefabricated albums are available from craft shops in both landscape and portrait shapes. If you want a cheap alternative, try using an ordinary ring binder or a large note book.

These albums are crafted from handmade papers and tissue, and enhanced with pressed leaves which have been sealed with PVA glue. The lettering is created using a rubber stamp.

DECORATING A COVER

The following pages offer a selection of finishes which can be used to enhance an album cover. Paper is a simple way to cover your album. Blockmounting and découpaging can be very effective and collage is so easy to do. Papers are available in so many different textures, colours and patterns that you can be as extravagant as you want. However, anything goes! Wonderful finishes are achieved with paint effects such as sponging and crackle finishing, and marbling is also a very effective technique.

If you are using paint on your album cover, you should seal the surface before you begin, using a coat of glaze medium, PVA glue, acrylic primer or spray varnish. Ask a good craft store for advice on their best sealant.

There is a glaze medium available which acts as a sealant, glue and light varnish. PVA glue can also be used.

Always remove excess glaze medium or PVA glue with damp paper towel.

Sponging

This technique creates a multicoloured background by building up sponged layers of colour. You can use a natural or synthetic sponge – depending on what you use, the effect will vary. Practice sponging on a spare piece of paper before you begin and remember to wear surgical gloves to protect your hands.

For this project, I have used an old Christmas card featuring a robin, but you could use any Christmas memento.

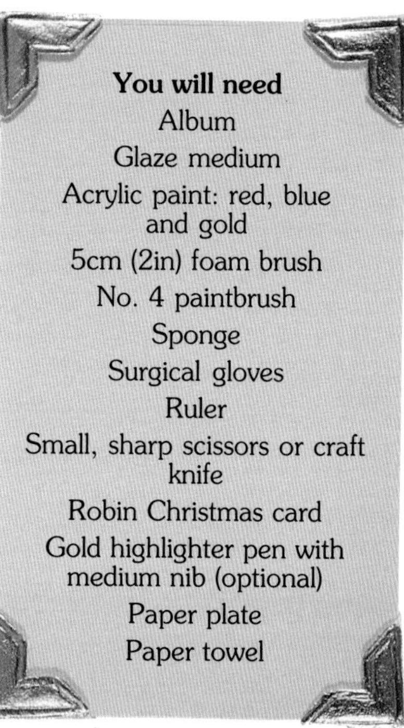

You will need

Album
Glaze medium
Acrylic paint: red, blue and gold
5cm (2in) foam brush
No. 4 paintbrush
Sponge
Surgical gloves
Ruler
Small, sharp scissors or craft knife
Robin Christmas card
Gold highlighter pen with medium nib (optional)
Paper plate
Paper towel

1 Use a foam brush to paint glaze medium over the front of the album – this will seal it (see page 21). Leave to dry. Repeat to cover the back and spine of the album.

2 Pour red acrylic paint on to a paper plate. Use a foam brush to apply the paint. Brush it in one direction to achieve a smooth finish. Leave to dry, then apply another coat.

Do not overload the brush when you are painting. Dab off excess paint on to paper towel.

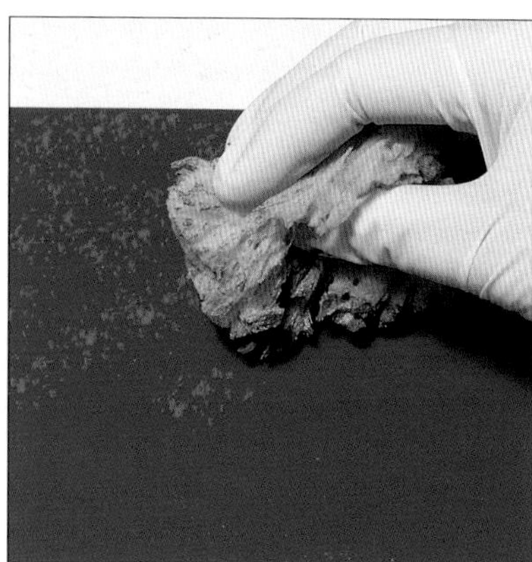

3 Pour blue paint on to the paper plate. Dip a dampened piece of sponge into the blue paint and then dab off the excess paint on a spare piece of paper. Now dab randomly over the surface of the album. Leave to dry.

4 Pour gold paint on to the paper plate. Use a clean piece of dampened sponge and gold paint to highlight some areas. Allow some of the background to show through. Leave to dry.

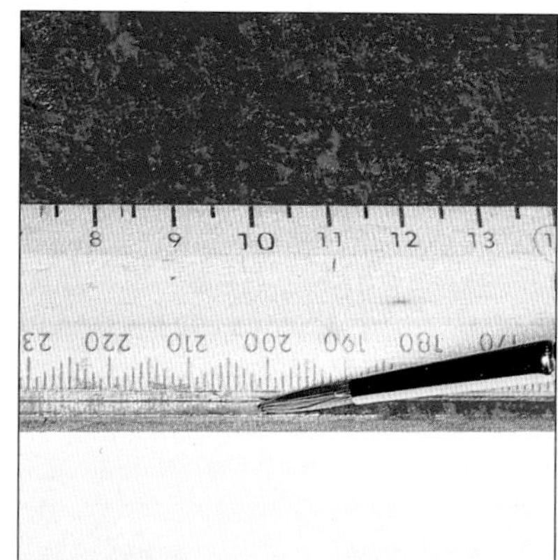

5 Use a No. 4 paintbrush and gold to paint around the edge of the front and back of the cover and around the spine. Use a ruler to achieve a thin, straight border. Wipe the ruler clean before repositioning it.

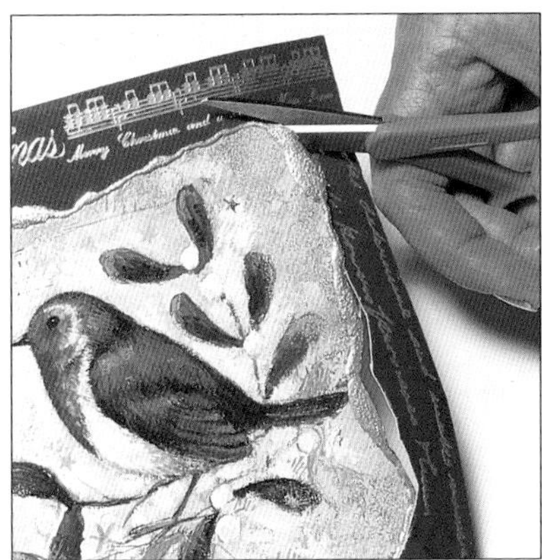

6 Cut out the robin using a pair of small, sharp scissors or a craft knife.

7 Attach the robin to the front cover using glaze medium. Press over the design with damp paper towel, then leave to dry.

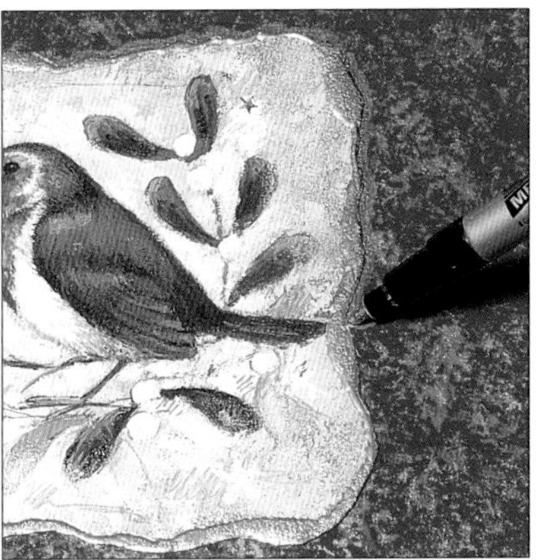

8 Outline the design using a gold highlighter pen or a No. 4 paintbrush and gold paint. Leave to dry. Apply a coat of glaze medium. Leave to dry.

Sponged Christmas Album

Blue and gold are sponged on to a red background to create a stunning Christmas album.

Quick and easy marbling

This is a simple but very effective technique that allows you to create unique effects – it is never possible to reproduce exactly the same pattern twice.

Marbling is best worked on an album which has a detachable front cover and is made from either wood or stiff card, as it will be immersed in water. Paper can also be marbled to create fabulous background papers, or paper to line the inside of your album with.

For this project, you need to immerse the album cover in a washing-up bowl of water and paint to create the marbled effect. Use surgical gloves for this project to protect your hands, and ensure the bowl is large enough to hold the album before you begin.

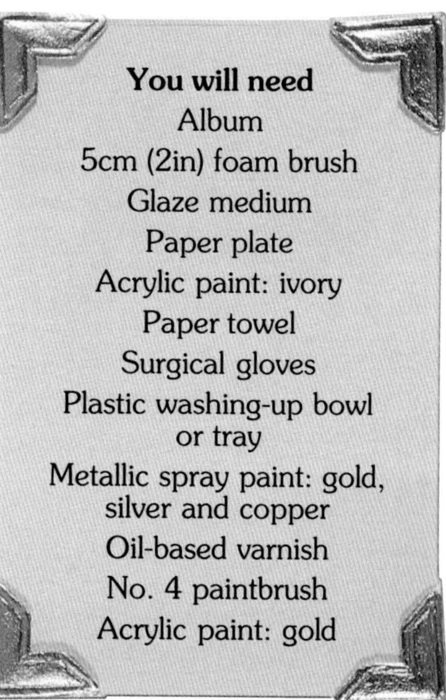

1 Seal the surface of the album cover (see page 22). Pour a small amount of ivory acrylic paint on to a paper plate. Use a foam brush to apply the paint. Leave to dry, then repeat for all the album pieces. Leave to dry before applying another coat.

When purchasing metallic paint, ensure that all colours are the same brand.

2 Half fill a plastic washing up bowl or tray with cold water. Spray a generous film of gold, silver and copper metallic paint on to the surface of the water. Leave for a few seconds for swirling patterns to form.

3 Gently lower the album cover, painted side down, into the water until it is completely immersed. Leave immersed for ten seconds.

4 Carefully lift the front cover out of the water and turn it the right way up. Leave to dry flat on paper towel.

5 Highlight the edges with gold paint (see page 22). Leave to dry before applying a coat of clear oil-based varnish.

Chocolate Fudge Vanilla Swirl Album

This would make a great children's party album. I have used silk ribbon to attach the spine to give an even more luxurious look.

Blockmounting

This project uses gift wrap to decorate an album cover. This technique is very easy and yet it produces stunning results. You can cover any album using blockmounting – even an ordinary ringbinder can be transformed. The variety of gift wrap available today means that you should be able to find something suitable for any theme. Save gift wrap from special occasions such as Christmas, weddings, birthdays or christenings.

This technique can be quite messy, so cover your work surface with newspaper or an old plastic table cloth before you begin.

To achieve a perfect edge to the blockmounted album, you 'cut' the gift wrap using sandpaper (see step 5).

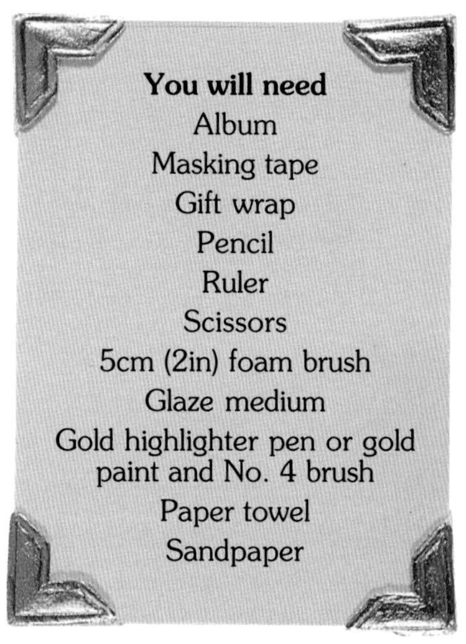

You will need

Album
Masking tape
Gift wrap
Pencil
Ruler
Scissors
5cm (2in) foam brush
Glaze medium
Gold highlighter pen or gold paint and No. 4 brush
Paper towel
Sandpaper

Wedding Album

This album is covered using gift wrap from a wedding present. The spine is decorated using the crackle finishing technique shown on pages 28–29.

1 Use masking tape to secure the gift wrap, printed side down, on to your work surface to stop it curling. Place the album cover on top of the gift wrap and draw a line approximately 1cm (½in) larger all round than the front of the album. Repeat for the back. Cut along the drawn lines.

2 Use a foam brush to apply a coat of glaze medium to each printed side of gift wrap – this will strengthen the paper and prevent curling while you are working. Leave to dry for about ten minutes, then apply another coat. Leave to dry.

3 Brush glaze medium over the surface of the front cover, and over the back of the gift wrap. Gently place the paper on top of the album and ease the gift wrap into position, leaving an even border of gift wrap all around the album. Repeat with the back cover.

4 Smooth out any air bubbles and wipe away excess glaze medium using damp paper towel.

5 Use sandpaper to remove excess gift wrap from the edges of the album. Work from right to left using brisk, sharp movements. Highlight around the edges with a gold highlighter pen or a small brush and gold paint.

Use medium or fine sandpaper depending on the thickness of your gift wrap.

Crackle finishing

Crackle finishing is a technique that is worked using a two-part glaze. The glaze reacts to create cracks, and these cracks are then highlighted with oil paint. It is essential that oil-based paint is used to bring up these cracks. Water-based paint will react with the top coat to leave a very sticky mess, like glue.

This popular finish looks great when fused with artwork. There are lots of different images you could use, including magazine cuttings, seed packets or artwork from a child's colouring book. Alternatively, try using photocopies of your own photographs, sealed with glaze medium.

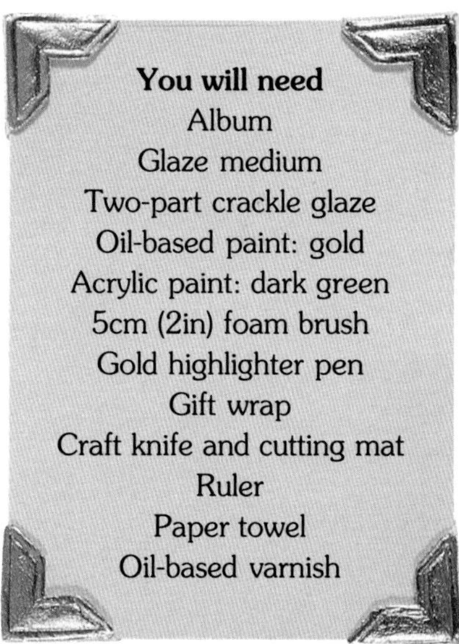

You will need

Album
Glaze medium
Two-part crackle glaze
Oil-based paint: gold
Acrylic paint: dark green
5cm (2in) foam brush
Gold highlighter pen
Gift wrap
Craft knife and cutting mat
Ruler
Paper towel
Oil-based varnish

Festive album

Crackle finish gives an old-fashioned look to your album.

1 Seal the album (see page 22). Apply a coat of dark green acrylic paint using a foam brush. Leave to dry, then apply another coat evenly. Leave to dry.

2 Cut shapes out of the gift wrap paper using a craft knife and ruler. Adhere in place with glaze medium. Remove any air bubbles or excess medium by rubbing gently over images with damp paper towel. Leave to dry.

3 Apply the base coat of crackle glaze using a foam brush. Leave to dry for approximately thirty minutes, then apply the top coat of crackle glaze. This time, leave to dry for approximately eight hours – the cracks should appear during drying.

4 Gently rub oil-based gold paint into the cracks with paper towel. Use circular movements and work in small areas at a time.

5 Remove excess gold paint with paper towel. Leave the album to cure for approximately three days before sealing with an oil-based varnish or one recommended by the crackle glaze manufacturer.

Wedding album

The spine of this album is embellished with gold thread and heart charms. Two die-cut card hearts are rubber stamped and embossed in gold. A collage of torn handmade paper, dried flowers, silk petals and glitter glue complete the decoration.

MAKING AN ALBUM

Anyone can go out and buy an album (see page 20), but you will feel such pride and satisfaction if you handcraft one yourself. This project demonstrates how to create an inexpensive album out of recycled card. I show you how to make a plain album, but you can personalise the album to suit any occasion (see the wedding album opposite).

Materials used for album front covers do not necessarily have to be acid-free, but the inside covers need to be lined with acid-free paper if they are closing on to photographs. However, you could get round this by using the first page of your album for journaling about the events that follow, and using the last page as an index.

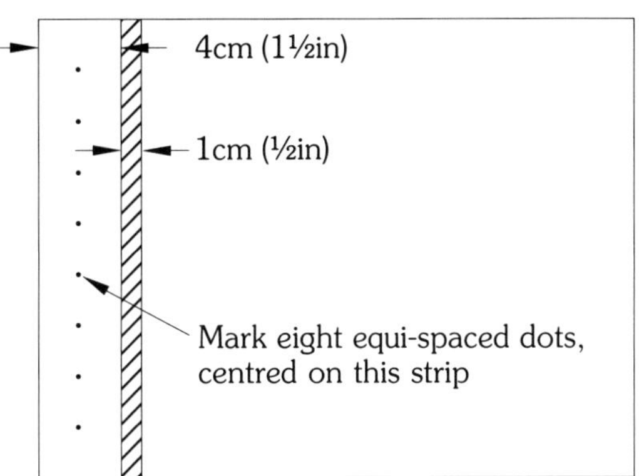

1 Copy this diagram carefully on to a 30 x 23cm (12 x 9in) rectangle of stiff card.

2 Cut out and discard the shaded segment of card as shown in the diagram. You are now left with the front cover and the spine.

3 Place the front cover and spine on top of the other piece of stiff card. Position them carefully to leave a gap where you cut out the narrow strip of card. Place a length of masking tape over the gap. Tape the front cover and the spine together then pick them up and wrap the tape around the inside to create a 'hinge'.

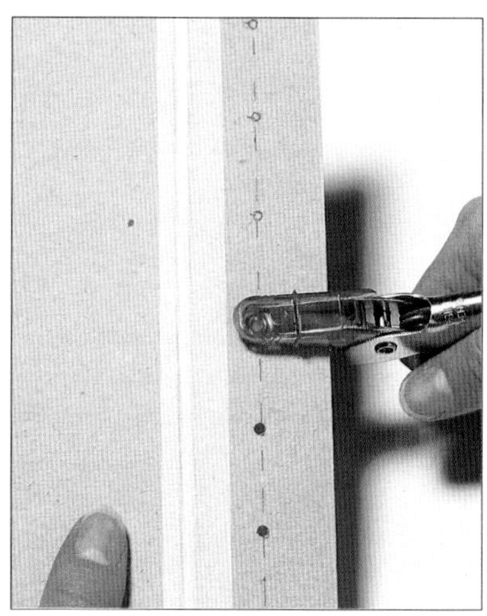

4 Position a hole punch over one of the eight marks in the centre of the spine. Punch out a hole, then repeat until all the holes are punched out. Use the spine as a template to mark and punch out holes on the back cover.

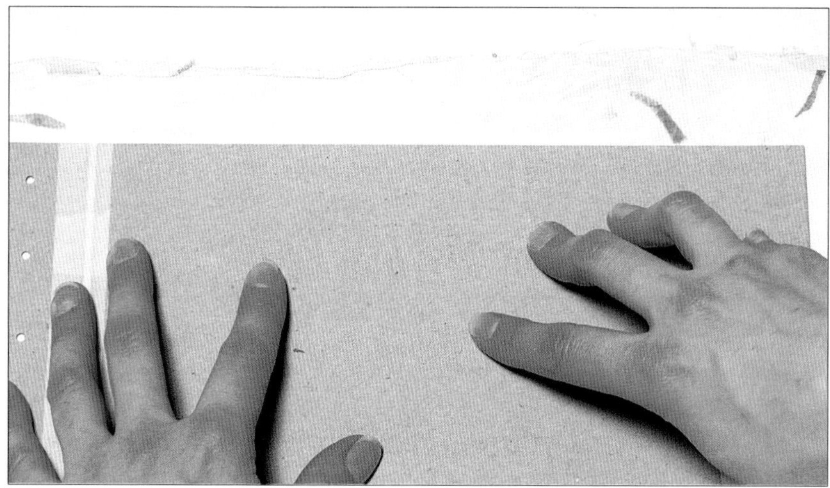

5 Cut out a piece of handmade petal paper 2.5cm (1in) larger all round than the front cover. Use a foam brush to apply glaze medium to the right side of the front cover and the wrong side of the petal paper. Place the cover on top of the petal paper and press down to stick it in place. Repeat this technique for the back cover.

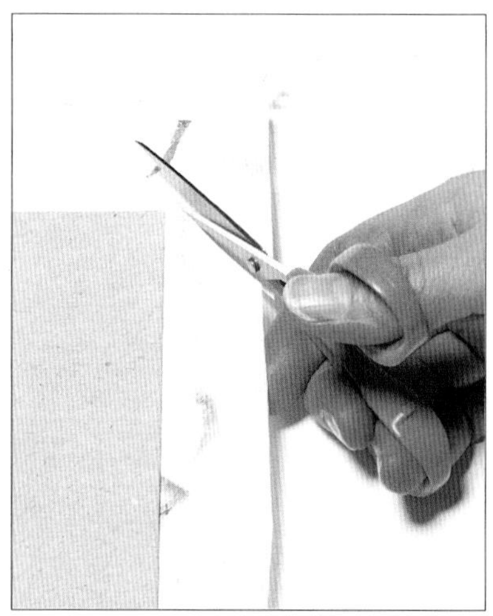

6 Cut the petal paper across each of the corners as shown. Do not cut right up to the card, but leave a gap of about 2–3mm (⅛in).

7 Pierce through the holes previously made in the front and back cover, using the tip of a pencil.

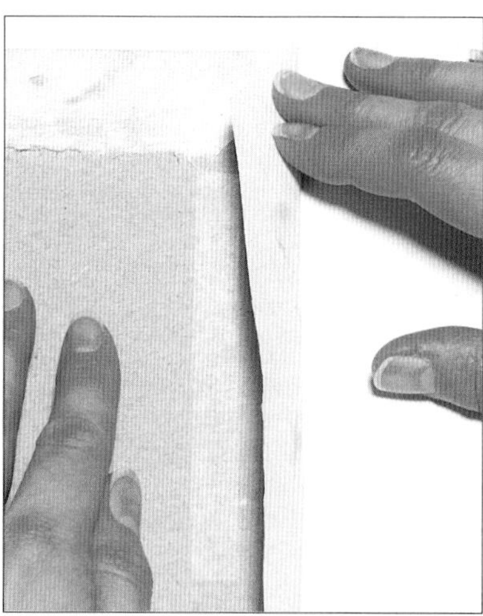

8 Apply strips of double-sided tape around the edge of the card. Fold back the petal paper around the edge of the card and press in place. Repeat on the back cover.

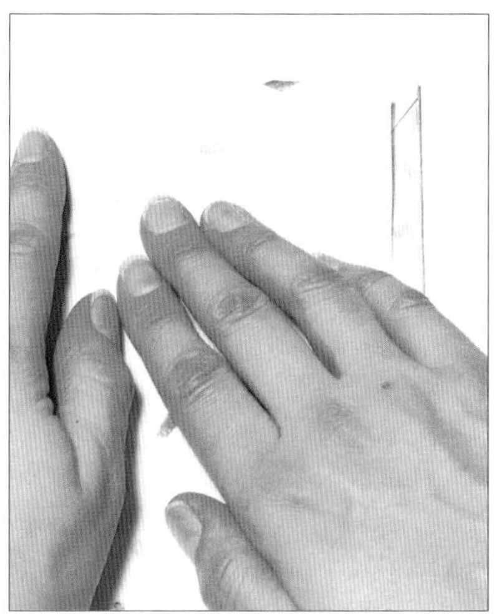

9 Cut out two pieces of petal paper approximately 0.5cm (¼in) smaller all round than the front and back cover. Use glaze medium to glue a piece on to the insides of the front and back covers to line them.

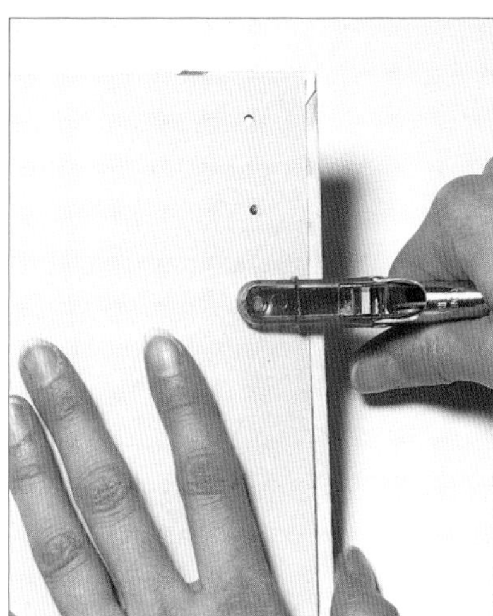

10 Re-punch holes through both covers. Position an album page against the front cover and line it up. Use the cover as a guide to locate a hole at the back of the cover. Position the hole punch in the hole, then punch the page. Continue, until you have punched through all the holes. Repeat for all the other album pages.

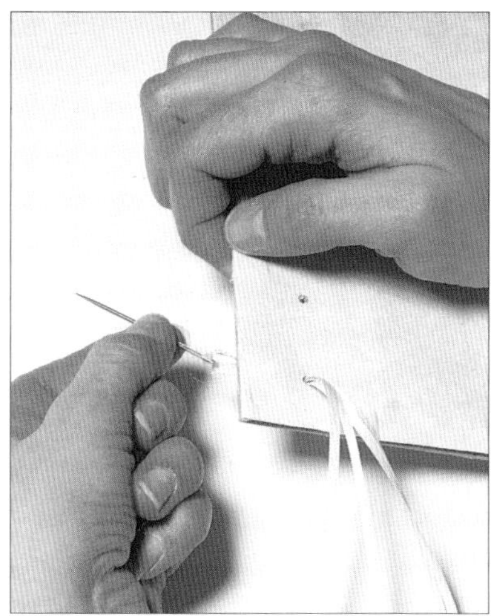

11 Assemble the album, sandwiching the pages in between the front and back covers. Line up all corresponding holes. Thread a tapestry needle with two lengths of coordinating ribbon. Thread the ribbon through the holes, starting at the bottom and leaving approximately 15cm (6in) of ribbon. Work the needle from the front to the back.

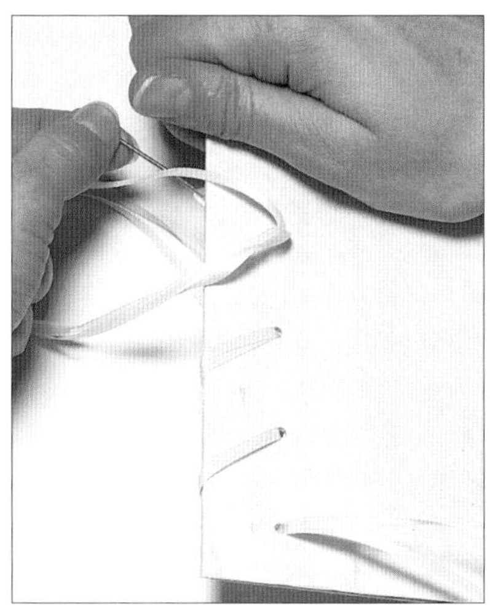

12 Continue working from front to back along the side of the album until you reach the top.

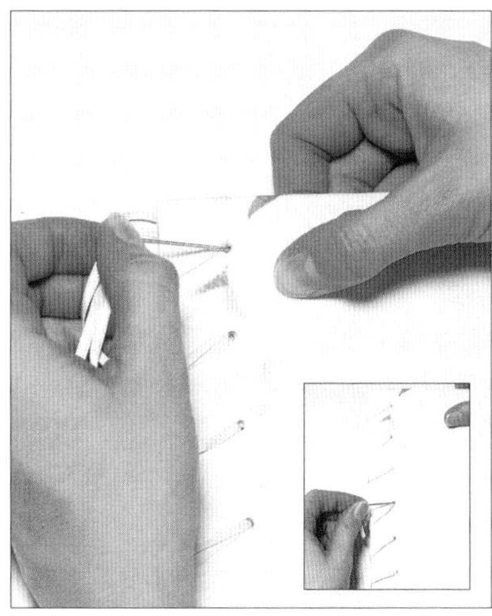

13 Work one horizontal stitch at the top of the album. Bring the needle around vertically to create another stitch at a right angle to the last one. Continue back down the edge, working from the front to the back to form a criss-cross pattern.

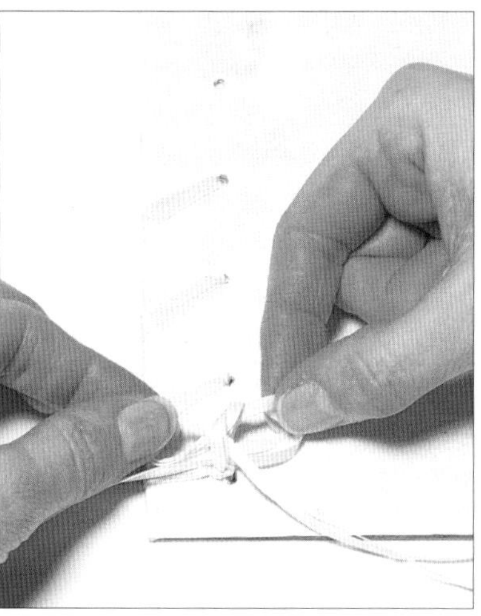

14 When you complete the last stitch, bring the ribbon through from the back and tie it to the ribbon at the front with a knot. Now tie a bow and trim the ends of the ribbon.

Background Papers

Background papers are used to create a setting for your photographs, to complement the page and to extend the theme of the memorabilia. You can have great fun creating your own backgrounds. For example, on a birthday page, you could include real streamers, balloons and gift wrap, and images of candles and presents. You could use techniques covered elsewhere in this book to create the background, or you could experiment to discover other ways of adding colour. For instance, wiping over a piece of white card with a used teabag will create a natural antique effect that might be appropriate for old sepia photographs.

You do not have to make your own background papers. There are many stores that supply a wonderful range of plain and patterned papers in different sizes. Beautiful effects such as bright splashes of colour or subtle tones, can be simply combined with photographs to create a truly memorable page.

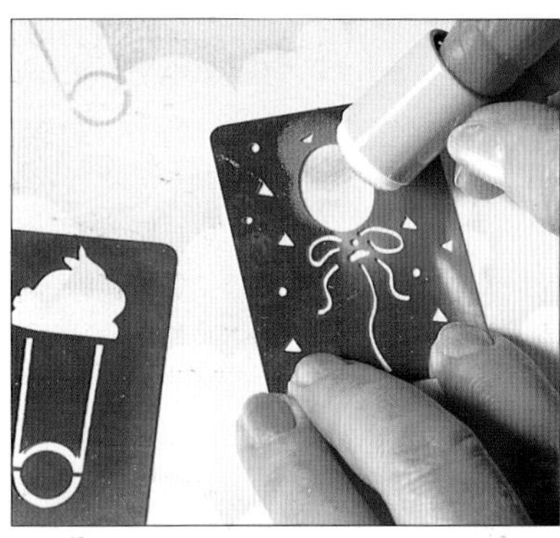

A sponge dauber is dabbed on to a pink ink cube then excess ink is removed on a piece of scrap paper. The sponge is pressed on to a cloud stencil and through to the background paper. The cloud image is repeated and then a balloon and safety-pin stencil are used. This time, excess ink is not removed, making the colour stronger.

These won First Prize at the Garden Festival!

I love to sit quietly listening to the birds reflecting on life especially when the sun is out

My Sanctuary

Where I take my book and coffee to escape from the busy world.

Our Garden = 1996 =

Blackie, our pet rabbit having his early breakfast of dry bread.

Fern stamps are dabbed on to either a light or dark green ink pad and used to stamp a pattern to create a background paper. The ferns around the edge are stamped partially going off the page. Butterfly stickers are then applied on top of and in between the stamped ferns. The butterflies around the edge are applied partially going off the page; they are then trimmed with a craft knife.

Sam the dolphin

You can write on a cut-out shape. Here, a dolphin has been traced on to coloured paper and cut out.

You can write on an oval shape cut out from a template (see page 62). Try spiralling the writing so that you end up filling the entire oval (this is a good way of disguising poor handwriting!).

You can write around a cut-out shape. Here, the writing follows the curve of a wave.

JOURNALING

Journaling brings an album to life. It is amazing how quickly our memories fade, so try to include the following information on an album page: the date, the place, the people featured and the reason the photograph was taken, i.e. 3 June 1998 at Chessington Zoo with Matthew and Owen on Owen's third birthday. You can also record favourite quotes from your children, poetry, songs, sayings and special thoughts.

There is a significant range of acid-free, light-fast, fade-resistant and waterproof pens on the market. These are available in an incredible range of colours, and with various nib sizes suitable for different writing. Luminous coloured pens can be used as highlighters and can look very effective on dark-coloured papers.

If you make a mistake when you are journaling, you can cut out a shape to complement your page, journal on to the shape, and then glue it over the mistake. You will find an easy writing template and practice sheet on pages 60–61 so you can avoid mistakes and achieve better results. You do not, of course, have to use my suggested style. Experiment to create your own unique lettering.

I think that it is best to let children do their own journaling, as this looks so much more realistic – and even spelling mistakes tell a story! Likewise, you may think your own handwriting is awful, but it still says something about you. However, if you do not feel confident enough to hand journal, experiment with using computer lettering printed on to recycled or handmade papers.

Sketch out all your journaling in light pencil first. You can then ensure you get the spacing between each letter and between each word correct before using pen. Any remaining pencil marks can be erased with a plastic eraser.

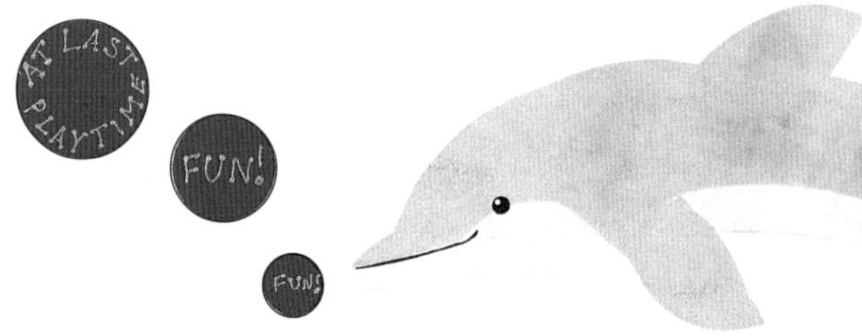

You can make your characters talk by creating speech bubbles and writing within these.

Making a splash

Journaling is worked on to splash shapes and a dolphin shape, and around a wave shape. Little whales are punched out and mounted between some of the journaling. The photographs are cropped and fish are punched out of the unwanted edges of the photographs.

Mounting

You can improve the look of photographs dramatically by fixing them on to acid-free paper or card mounts. Always use acid-free glue, acid-free double-sided adhesive tape or photo corners to mount your photographs. Try to choose mounts that complement the photograph itself, in terms of colour, theme or mood.

You can decorate a mount. For example, you could add successive layers of card, cut around the edge with decorative scissors or tear the edge roughly by hand. Decorative punches can be used on borders and corners of mounts, and to create decorative effects such as lace. You can punch out abstract motifs, or images such as teddy bears, hearts or stars. If you do this, you can decorate the album page with the images that you have punched out.

Place a clean piece of acid-free paper over a photograph immediately after gluing it on to a mount. Rub over the surface with your hands to smooth out any air bubbles. The paper will serve to protect your photograph as you do this.

A mount can be cut with decorative scissors. Keep the outer edge of the scissors parallel with the edge of the paper in order to ensure a straight line.

A mount can be torn to create an interesting edge. Tear the paper towards you if you want the plain edge of the paper to show, and away from you if you want a clean edge.

The corners of a mount can be decorated using a decorative punch.

Baby face

Try using découpage stickers (see page 44) to 'mount' your piece. Even though stickers say they are acid-free it is often safer not to place them directly on to a photograph. Here, I have used photocopies rather than original photographs.

Patient Vicky

You can mount on coloured pieces of card that complement the colours in the photo.

Sunflower

Try mounting an image, then cutting around it to create a mount that complements the shape of the image.

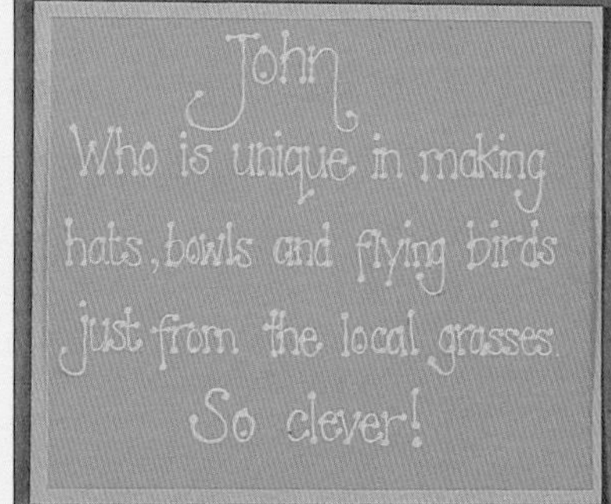

Clever John

You can mount coloured journaling on coloured card to make it more pronounced, and then create a double mount using the same colours.

Sunny days

This page uses bright yellow mounts to create a sunny effect. The sunflower is photocopied from a magazine and the bee, beehive and bear stickers are highlighted with a pen (see page 44). Faces are drawn on the buttons using a permanent pen, then a highlighter is used to add petals and transform them into flowers.

The Lazy Daisy Days of Summer!

There is a bit missing!

Daisy the star in my eyes!

Where is my icecream?

There is a bee in my icecream!

Daisy and Matthew
Enjoying their icecreams and wearing their new Sunglasses
October '90

Road to Hana

Multicoloured mounts add even more colour to this tropical page. The leaves are collaged from photographs of real plants. The letters are highlighted with little dashes to make them stand out, and tropical bird stickers add the finishing touch.

Sailing around Hawaii

Here, background paper is created by stamping with silver ink and the photographs are then mounted directly on top. A photograph of a sunrise is cut out in the shape of a sun, using a template. Journaling is added on to anchor- and fish-shaped pieces of coloured card.

DECORATING PAGES

Easy découpage

You can buy découpage sheets that contain pre-cut images which are acid- and lignin-free and which have adhesive on the back. Alternatively, you can cut out your own images and then glue them down. Here I have used the technique of découpage with stickers. Stickers are an easy way to decorate or theme a page and there are many different types available.

To make stickers repositionable, you can gently pat the sticky side on to a piece of scrap fabric several times; this helps to weaken the adhesive.

Do not put stickers directly on to photographs, but work on photocopies instead.

You can embellish stickers by adding details, such as grass, using a pen.

You can use individual stickers to embellish a page and create a theme.

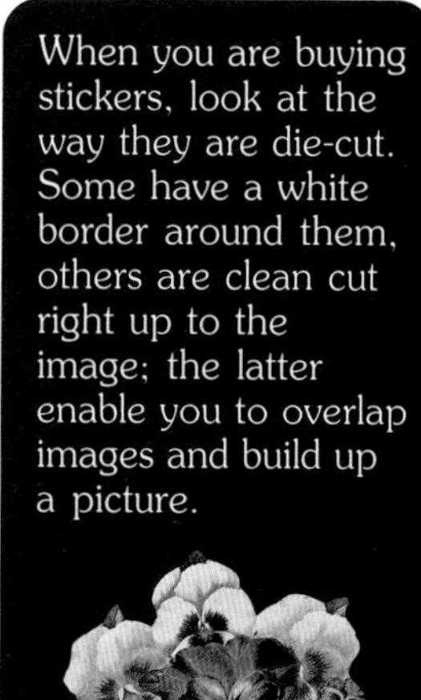

When you are buying stickers, look at the way they are die-cut. Some have a white border around them, others are clean cut right up to the image; the latter enable you to overlap images and build up a picture.

A border can be applied around a page to decorate it, using individual stickers to create a solid line. You can also use stickers to build up an oval border. Tear off small sections then ease them gently around the corner. Try building up borders and corners using both small and large images.

Grandparents
This page was created using découpage stickers to build up a mount around the photographs.

Rubber stamping

Rubber stamping is a fast and colourful way to enhance a page. This technique can be used to create backgrounds (see pages 35 and 43), frames for your photographs (see page 59) and to theme your page. Here, I have used horse stamps to pick up the theme introduced by the photographs.

You will need
Rubber stamp of horses
Black ink pad
Recycled paper
Coloured pencils: two shades of brown

1 Press the horse stamp on to a black stamp pad to cover it with ink. Stamp directly on to a piece of recycled paper.

2 Colour in the image with coloured pencils and two shades of brown.

3 Tear roughly around the stamped image to produce an uneven line.

Recycled paper can be quite absorbent. As a result, your stamping may occasionally be faint, or lines may be broken. If this happens, you can touch up the image or lettering using an ultra-fine black pen.

Vicky's big day

Photographs are cropped and mounted on to background paper that looks like wooden fencing. Computer-generated journaling is printed out on to recycled card. The card is torn roughly out and stuck in place.

Moonlight Madness
In Riding a Horse We Borrow Freedom
Helen Thompson
Vicky Sep '97
A first for Vicky competing in Hunter Trials at Borde Hill, West Sussex on Moonlight Madness.
Ardingly Riding Club
Placed
First

Simple stenciling

Stenciling is an excellent technique for decorating album pages. It can be used to create borders around a page and around a central photograph.

You can create different effects with stenciling simply by filling in the lines, or leaving them open. The stencils are held in place on your page using masking tape. You can remove some of the adhesive from the masking tape by gently patting the sticky side on to a piece of scrap fabric several times. This will prevent your background paper from being damaged when you remove the tape.

This project also uses simple découpage to enhance the effect. Rose stickers have been used, but you could use fruit or other motifs, depending on the theme of your page.

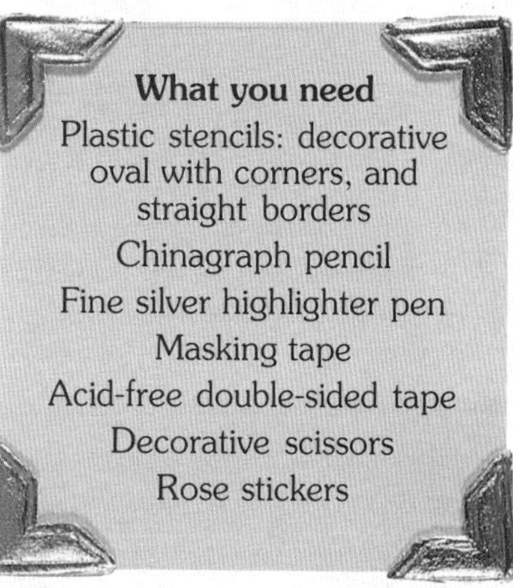

What you need

Plastic stencils: decorative oval with corners, and straight borders
Chinagraph pencil
Fine silver highlighter pen
Masking tape
Acid-free double-sided tape
Decorative scissors
Rose stickers

Victorian Elegance
Stenciling is simple to do, and it can be used to create an elegant effect. Gold or silver highlighter pens can be used on a dark background for a really striking contrast. Here, the journaling is worked on a small rectangle of paper which is then positioned over the stenciling at the bottom of the page.

2 Position the stencil over the album page and tape it in place with masking tape. Go around the stencil lines with a silver highlighter pen.

1 Tape the photograph on to your work surface with a little masking tape. Lay the stencil over the photograph and tape it in place. Draw in the simple line border around the central image using a chinagraph pencil. Cut out the photograph using decorative scissors.

3 Remove the stencil and fill in some or all of the lines with a silver highlighter.

4 Reposition the oval stencil so that the corner decoration can be penned in. Use the silver highlighter to fill in the stencil lines. Use a separate stencil for the straight border lines, or mark them in using a ruler.

5 Apply rose stickers around the stenciled design. Glue the photograph into the central oval.

Stencil embossing

Stencil embossing produces a subtle effect and gives a wonderfully delicate feel to any project. If you want to make more of an impact, you can enhance your embossing with the addition of a little colour or glitter, as shown here.

I have used a lightbox in this demonstration, but you could hold the stencil up to a sunny window and place the linen card on top so that the images shows through the stencil. Alternatively, place a lamp under a glass-top coffee table and place your card and stencil on top of the glass.

You will need
Brass flower stencil
Light box
Masking tape
Linen card
Oval template
Embossing tool
Pink ink cube
Sponge dauber

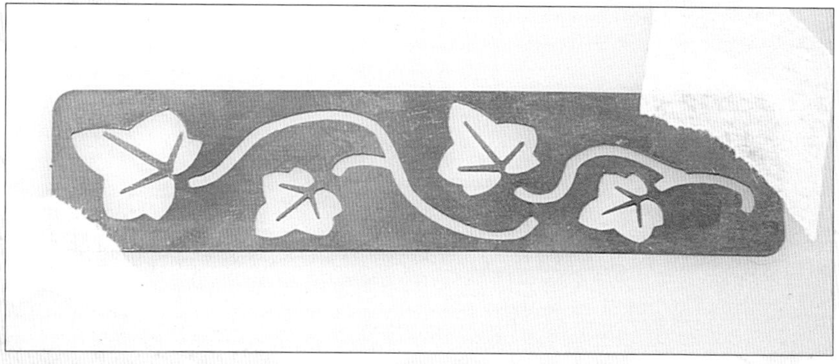

1 Tape the stencil on to a light box with masking tape.

2 Use the template on page 62 to draw an oval on to linen card. Cut out and discard the oval. Place the card frame, right side down, over the stencil. Follow the outline of the image with the embossing tool, pressing down hard. Move the stencil around the oval frame and continue embossing until the frame is complete.

3 Turn the card over so that it is right side up. Place the stencil on top of the raised design, exactly matching the embossed areas. Dab a sponge dauber on to a pink ink cube then lightly pat it over the raised areas to colour the image.

Wedding Day

Stencil embossing works well for wedding, christening and Christmas pages – try using a snowflake stencil to create a wonderful winter scene. Glitter glue can be added over embossing to create sparkle. If you want this effect, remember that glitter can migrate and may scratch your photograph – it is therefore best to work with a photocopy rather than an original.

Collage

Collage is a technique that involves overlapping different papers, cards and other materials to complement each other and form a picture or background. You can have great fun gathering together a variety of memorabilia suitable for collage. Here, I began with a selection of party hats, tinsel, old Christmas cards, tags and ribbons. I arranged the pieces until I was happy with the composition of the design, and then glued it in place, working from the top down.

There are lots of possibilities for collage. You could use birthday, wedding, christening, holiday or school days memorabilia. You can build up a collage or background paper using photocopies of relevant items – for example, an exercise book, sports kit, school tie, lunch box, bus tickets and pencil case would be perfect for an album about school days.

When collaging, always use acid-free glue or acid-free double-sided tape to attach memorabilia and photographs.

A selection of Christmas memorabilia.

OPPOSITE

Christmas party

This background is collaged using a selection of the Christmas memorabilia shown above. Christmas photographs are mounted on to old Christmas cards and placed on top of the collage. Journaling is adding on to holly leaves cut from green card.

Christmas Wishes
Merry Christmas
Richard dressed as Robin Hood ready for his fancy dress competition
Merry Christmas
Laura & Richard Christmas 1991
Laura practising her flute for a Christmas competition at school. She also came 2nd in her Christmas hat competition!

Parchment craft

Parchment craft is an embossing technique used with transluscent paper. The paper can also be cut to create delicate patterns. Although it is a little time-consuming, it is extremely rewarding and it will give a wonderfully delicate and intricate look to your work.

This project uses white and gold waterproof ink. There are many types available, including one designed specifically for this craft. White ink should be shaken thoroughly before use, and the top of the bottle should be replaced as soon as you have finished using it, to prevent the ink from thickening.

You will need
Embossing mat
Parchment paper
Masking tape
Mapping pen
Waterproof ink: white and gold
Embossing tool
Single needle tool
Small, sharp parchment craft scissors

Baby blue

The parchment pocket is attached to the background card by gluing down the bottom and side edges. A lock of the baby's hair is tucked into the top of the pocket and ribbon bows are added to the corners.

The parchment frame for the photograph and the rattle are created using the same techniques as the pocket. They are coloured with waterproof inks and pencils, and the frame is also rubber stamped with black permanent ink.

Gingham paper is cut with decorative scissors to create a border at the top and bottom of the page. Train and cloud punches are used to add the finishing touches and journaling is added on to a large cloud shape.

Pattern for parchment pocket

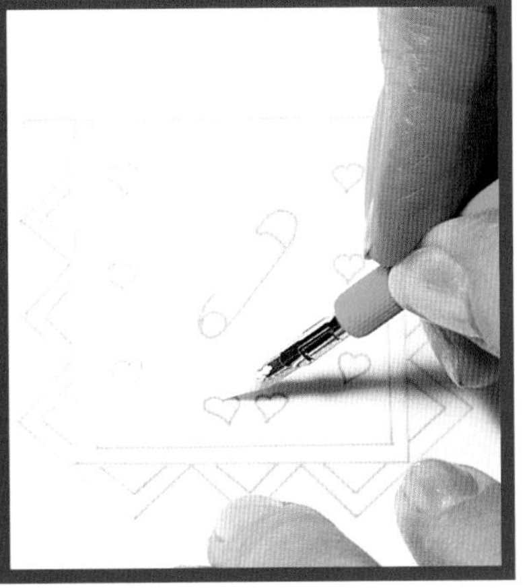

1 Photocopy the pattern provided, increasing or reducing the size to fit your album page. Secure a piece of parchment paper over the image using masking tape. Trace the design using a mapping pen and white waterproof ink.

2 Fill in the safety pin using gold ink.

3 Place the parchment paper right side down on an embossing mat. Use the embossing tool to emboss between all the straight lines. Do not over over-emboss, or the paper will stiffen. Emboss the hearts and safety-pin head.

4 Turn the parchment paper right side up on the embossing mat. Perforate around the inside and outside of the border using a single needle tool. Work the tool up and down like a sewing machine.

5 Snip the perforated edges with small, sharp parchment craft scissors. Carefully remove the small triangles of parchment paper to create a delicate edge.

MORE IDEAS

The following pages give a few more ideas about how to theme and organise your pages to coordinate with your photographs.

Ice Storm
These wonderful photographs are mounted on to holographic background paper and I have used glitter and die-cut and punched-out snowflakes to continue the theme. The background is stenciled with a silver ink cube and sticker lettering is used to enhance the journaling.

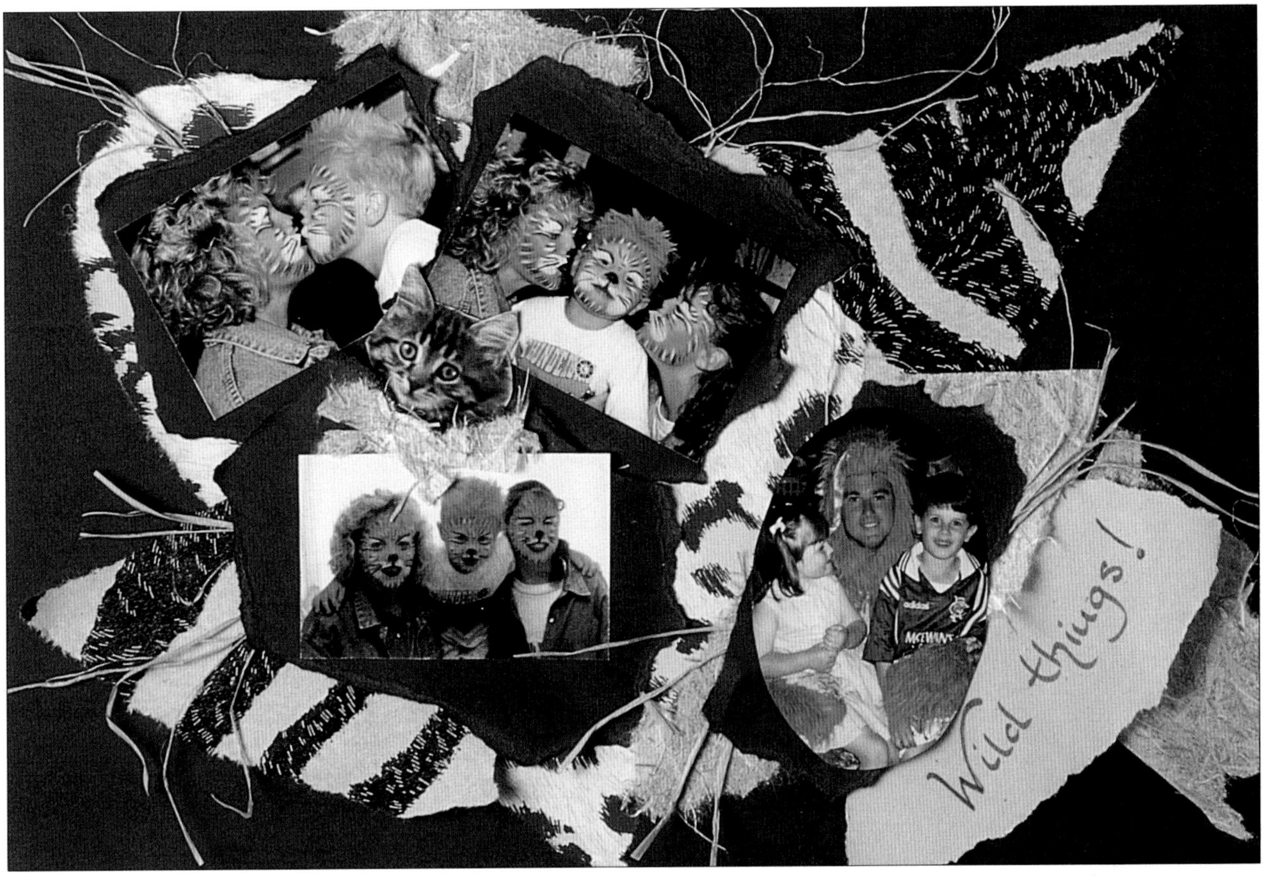

Wild things

These strips of dramatic background papers were used to tie in with the colourful photographs and the animal theme of the page. Raffia provides the finishing touch and is used to suggest whiskers.

Emma

This picture cried out for a Victorian look, so heavily embossed gold frames were used – one for the photograph, the other for the journaling.

Michael and Jeremy after a sand pit fight – what a mess!

Fun in the Garden

The little boy featured in these photographs is affectionately referred to as 'a toad' by his mum. This page picks up on the toad theme and uses découpage stickers to embellish the photographs. The bubble photograph is enhanced by bubbles drawn on to the background. Simple pre-cut paperlace frames surround each photograph. Journaling is added directly on to the page.

Sand pit fight

A mount can be extended to make room for journaling. Here, sand-coloured card is used to complement the theme of the picture. Sea shell stickers are used to adhere the mount to the background.

A special day
Rubber stamps are used to created a floral feel to this wedding page. Pressed flowers from the posies embellish the page further.

Best friends are forever
This background paper is created by masking the middle section with a sticky notelet and using a ruler and toning coloured pens to draw lines. The notelet is removed to leave a white frame to 'mount' the photograph. Journaling is added and single pansy stickers are overlapped to create a corner design.

Friends
These frames are rubber stamped and gold embossed. They are then coloured with watercolour pencils, and a craft knife is used to cut away jagged diamond shapes for the photographs to fit behind. The flowers and butterflies are punched out and decorative scissors are used on background paper to create an edge to the page. Tassels are added in coordinating colours.

EASY WRITING TEMPLATE

This easy writing template will help you to improve your writing skills. Practise the lettering until you get the spacing between the letters looking natural and you feel confident to journal directly on to your album.

ABCDEFGH
IJKLMNOPQ
RSTUVWXYZ
abcdefghijkl
mnopqrstuv
wxyz .,?!&()
1234567890

Practise makes perfect

Photocopy these guide lines on to tracing paper. You can then place the tracing paper on top of the writing template and practice the letters. The uppercase letters should be worked between the wide solid lines, and the lowercase letters between a dashed top line and lower solid line. Always complete words before adding dots to your journaling.

PHOTOGRAPH TEMPLATES

You can enlarge or reduce any of these templates on a photocopier to fit your photographs.

Glossary

Acid causes paper and photographs to deteriorate. This ageing process is slowed down significantly if acid is removed during manufacture. Acid-free products include glue, papers, pens and photograph corners.

Archival quality indicates materials which have undergone laboratory tests to determine that their acid content is stable.

Background papers are available in a range of colours and patterns. They can be used as a background for a themed page, or heavyweight papers can be used as pages.

Blockmounting is a technique which uses glue and gift wrap to decorate a surface.

Crackle finishing is a technique which uses two types of glaze to produce small cracks on a surface. The cracks are then highlighted with paint to produce an aged look.

Cropping is the cutting or trimming of a photograph to retain the essential parts. It is possible to crop in a variety of shapes using templates.

Die-cuts are cut-out shapes. They can be traced from an existing image, or templates can be used to create the shape.

Journaling simply means writing. It is an important part of a memory album and can be handwritten, worked with rubber stamps or sticker lettering, or it can be computer generated.

Lignin is the bonding element which holds wood fibres together. It causes paper to change colour and become brittle. Lignin can be removed during manufacture to make the paper safe. Most paper, other than newsprint, is lignin-free.

Memorabilia is a collection of articles from special occasions, i.e. air tickets, coins, wine labels, menus and theatre tickets.

Mounting involves sticking a photograph on to coloured card to frame it. Alternatively, a photograph can be placed directly on the page using photograph corners.

Templates can be made of plastic or card. You can make your own, or you can buy them. They come in various shapes, i.e. squares, ovals, circles and hearts. Themed templates are also available, i.e. Christmas trees, stockings, candles and snowflakes.

INDEX

771 Wright, Maggie.
WRI All you need to know
c.1 about making memory
albums $10.95

acid-free 8, 11, 14, 18, 31, 38, 40, 44, 63
adhesive stick 8
album
  choosing an 20
  covering an 8, 10, 11
  making an 6, 10, 31–33
album cover, decorating an 6, 21
archival quality 11, 63

blockmounting 6, 10, 21, 26–27, 63

card 11, 16, 31, 38
collage 6, 21, 42, 52–53
chinagraph pencil 10, 15, 49
crackle finishing 6, 8, 10, 21, 26, 28–29, 63
crackle glaze 8, 28, 29, 63
craft knife 10, 15, 23, 29, 35, 59
cropping 6, 10, 15–17, 18, 63
cutting mat 10

découpage 6, 10, 21, 44–45, 48
die-cuts 30, 44, 56, 63
double-sided tape 8, 10, 32, 38

embossing 8, 30, 54, 57, 59
  stencil 6, 10, 50–51
embossing mat 8, 55
embossing tool 8, 50, 55
eraser, plastic 10, 15, 36

foam brush 10, 22, 24, 27, 29, 32

gift wrap 10, 26, 27
glaze medium 8, 22, 23, 27, 32, 33
glitter 10, 30, 51, 56
gloves, surgical 10, 22, 24
gluing 8, 21

ink cube 10, 34, 50, 56
ink pad 10, 35, 46

journaling 6, 8, 10, 11, 31, 36–37, 40, 43, 46, 48, 52, 54, 56, 58, 59, 60–61, 63

lightbox 10, 50
lignin-free 8, 44, 63
mapping pen 8, 55
marbling 6, 8, 10, 21, 23, 24–25
masking tape 10, 27, 31, 48, 49, 50, 55
memorabilia 12, 13, 52, 63
mounting 6, 10, 11, 16, 19, 38–43, 45, 58, 63

needle 10, 33

paint
  acrylic 10, 22, 23, 29
  metallic spray 8, 24
  oil-based 10, 28, 29
paintbrush 10, 22, 23
palette 10
paper 11, 21, 24, 38
  background 6, 11, 19, 24, 34–35, 56, 57, 59, 63
  handmade 10, 20, 30, 32, 33
  parchment 8, 10, 55
paperlace 19, 58
paper towel 10, 21, 22, 23, 27, 29
parchment craft 6, 8, 54–55
pencils 10, 32, 46, 54
pens 8, 10, 36
photocopying 14, 15, 18–19, 40, 44, 51
photographs
  damaged 18
  duplicate prints of 15, 18
  handling 14
  polaroid 15
  sepia 18, 34
  storing 14
  theming 12
photograph corners 10, 38, 63
punch
  decorative 10, 37, 38, 39, 54, 56, 59
  single hole 10, 32
PVA glue 8, 20, 21

red eyes, removing 14
ribbon 10, 25, 33, 54
rubber stamps 10, 20, 35
rubber stamping 6, 10, 30, 35, 43, 46–47, 54, 58, 59, 63
ruler 10, 22, 29, 49, 59

sandpaper 10, 26, 27
scalpel *see* craft knife
scissors 10, 23
  decorative 10, 38, 49, 54, 59
  parchment craft 10, 55
sealing 8, 21, 22, 24, 29
single needle tool 8, 10, 55
sponge 10, 22
sponge dauber 10, 34, 50
sponging 6, 10, 21, 22–23
stencils 8, 10, 50
stenciling 6, 10, 34, 48–49, 56
stencil embossing *see* embossing
stickers 10, 35, 40, 42, 44, 45, 48, 49, 56, 58, 59, 63

template 10, 15, 43, 63
  easy writing 36, 60
  photograph 62
tissue 11, 20

varnish, oil-based 8, 25, 29
varnishing 8, 21

washing-up bowl 24
waterproof ink 8, 54, 55
white spirit 8

Miniature album
The cover of this unusual miniature album is made from Christmas fabric and the photographs are reduced on a colour photocopier to fit.

DRIFTWOOD LIBRARY
OF LINCOLN CITY
801 S.W. Highway 101
Lincoln City, Oregon 97367